Modern Industrial World

Portugal

Neil Champion

Thomson Learning

New York

MODERN INDUSTRIAL WORLD

France

Germany

Japan

Portugal

Russia

Sweden

Cover: The outside of a modern shopping center in Lisbon.
Title page: A satellite dish, part of Portugal's modern communications
network, stands alongside a field of crops in Sintra, near Lisbon.
Contents page: Vineyards are found along the valley of the Douro
River in northern Portugal.

First published in the
United States in 1995 by
Thomson Learning
New York, NY

First published in Great Britain in 1995 by
Wayland (Publishers) Ltd.

Library of Congress Cataloging-in-Publication Data
Champion, Neil.
 Portugal / Neil Champion.
    p.   cm. —(Modern industrial world)
 Includes bibliographical references and index.
 ISBN 1-56847-435-0 (hc)
 1. Portugal—Description and travel—Juvenile literature.
2. Portugal—Economic conditions—Juvenile literature.
I. Title. II. Series.
DP526.5.C47   1995
946.904—dc20   95-17619

Printed in Italy

Contents

Background to a Nation

The fertile valley of the Douro River in northern Portugal. Dotted across this gentle landscape are quintas, *the wine estates that produce the grapes to make port.*

Portugal is a small country, about half the size of the state of Indiana. It is situated on the western edge of the European continent, facing the huge expanse of the Atlantic Ocean to the west, sharing a 746-mile border with Spain to the east. The landscape is diverse and beautiful, with mountains, plains, river valleys, and windswept coastal regions. In recent years it has attracted tourists by the thousands. This is especially true of the far south, the Algarve, with its Mediterranean climate of hot summers and warm winters and a wealth of stunning beaches and rocky coves.

PORTUGAL AT A GLANCE

Total area: 35,515 sq mi. This includes Portugal's island territories of Madeira and the Azores.
Population: 10,500,000.
Capital city: Lisbon.
Currency: Escudo (= 100 centavos).
Life expectancy for men: 71 years
Life expectancy for women: 78 years

JOINING THE EUROPEAN UNION

When Portugal joined the European Union (EU) in 1986, it was one of the poorest and least developed countries

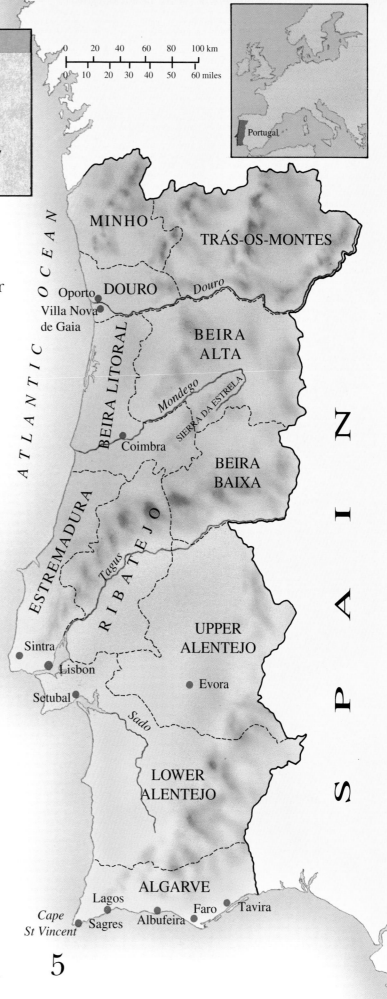

in Western Europe. It had only recently emerged from a right-wing dictatorship that had held power for nearly 50 years. It had done little in its years of power to keep up with the social, economic, and technological changes that had transformed the rest of Western Europe and made people's lives easier and more comfortable. The regime was conservative and outdated. The country remained essentially agricultural. Tourism started to make an impact in the 1960s, and has steadily developed since then. The right-wing regime was overthrown in 1974, making way for democracy and bringing many improvements to people's lives. But by the late 1980s, the Gross National Product (GNP) was only about $8,000 per person—two-thirds that of its neighbor, Spain.

5

A cork factory at Portalegre, in the Alentejo. This region of the country is very poor and has been slow to industrialize.

MODERNIZATION

Since 1986 a noticeable change has come about in the economy. The country has moved quickly to modernize and industrialize itself. It has done this partly with financial aid from the European Union. By the early 1990s, Portugal had the fastest growing economy in Europe. This was from a low starting point, but nonetheless it was a significant achievement. Foreign investment (which is a measure of the confidence other nations have in a country) doubled in 1989. The GNP growth was at a very healthy 5.5% in the same year.

Portugal has been modernizing ever since. Investment has gone into industries such as chemicals; textiles and clothing manufacturing; wood products; china and earthenware; road, office, and house building; and energy production (especially hydroelectric). Even so, Portugal remains more dependent on agriculture and tourism than other developed nations.

HOW PEOPLE ARE EMPLOYED	
Services (including tourism):	.49%
Industry, construction, and energy:	44%
Agriculture, forestry, and fishing:	.7%

6

There are very few mineral deposits apart from tungsten, copper, and tin. In spite of the diversity of crops, Portugal is plagued with poor soil and old-fashioned farming methods. Younger people have left the countryside to live abroad or in the towns and cities, where they can find work. This has brought problems to rural villages. Traditional ways of life are dying out with the older generation that is left behind, and the land is left unused.

Modern Portugal combines the old and the new, a fact seen in the gap between the older and the younger generations. Today's 20-year-old is interested in cars, computers, electronics, household appliances, and travel. Their parents or grandparents may still work a small farm

These women are harvesting the potato crop. Their children and grandchildren will probably leave for the cities, where there is more work.

The port wine industry

A traditional port wine barge on the Douro River at Oporto. Barges were used to transport the barrels of wine from the quintas *upriver to the lodges at Villa Nova de Gaia, where they were stored.*

Taylor's port wine lodge in Villa Nova de Gaia is the oldest in Portugal. It was established in 1692. The English claim the invention of port, which is wine with brandy added to it. They developed the vineyards of the Douro River, where they cultivated grapes, harvested them, and put them in barrels. These were taken

"For generations my family have lived here in the Douro valley. We have a small farm. We have always helped with the grape harvest in autumn. We still pick the fruit by hand as our parents did, but the money has never been very good." –Antonio Sequiera, farmer, and seasonal grape picker

and have no means of transport other than a donkey, no electricity, running water, or sanitation. Never having gone to school, they may be unable to read or write.

downstream on boats to the estuary and Oporto. The English controlled the industry for hundreds of years and are still actively involved today.

The different types of port are produced at the lodges. These include vintage, late-bottled vintage, ruby, and tawny. Port is drunk all over the world today. Its production makes up a significant part of the Portuguese wine trade.

"In the old days, the barrels were taken downriver to Oporto in lovely barges. You can still see them advertising the different companies –Taylors, Sandemans, Delaforce – as they bob up and down on the water outside the famous lodges. Today the barrels are taken down the winding road by truck. The trip is about 50 miles." **–Antonio Sequiera**

"The grapes have a hard time here in the upper Douro valley. The soil is tough and water can be 50 feet down. The climate is quite extreme for Portugal. The winters are cold – we often get snow. And the summers are long and hot inland. Because of this, few grapes grow on the vines, compared with French or Italian vines, say. But the ones that do grow have a great flavor and very thick skins."
–Antonio Sequiera

Portugal is now part of the modern industrial world, but traces of its recent poor and backward economy still reluctantly remain.

9

Portugal's Historical Development

The earliest signs of human activity were found in caves around Lisbon. These were sharpened stones that date back to 400,000 B.C. One of the first ancient civilizations to settle there was the Phoenician. They were a Mediterranean seafaring nation who built trading ports along the coast of Portugal. The Celts settled more permanently and built farms and villages from about 600 B.C.

THE ROMANS

The Romans arrived at the beginning of the second century A.D. and stayed for over six hundred years. Physical evidence of their presence can be seen in the remains of roads, bridges, and sites such as Evora and Conimbriga, which still have temples and and many buildings with the original structures. The Romans also left other legacies. Language is one of these. Portuguese comes from Latin, the language of the Romans.

The Roman temple at Evora is one of the best preserved ancient sites in Portugal.

THE MOORS

The next significant invasion came in the shape of the Moors, an Arabic people from North Africa. They arrived in Spain in 711 and quickly conquered all lands in the south, including what is today part of Portugal. "Algarve" is a Moorish word, meaning "the West." The Algarve became a Moorish kingdom and today there is still a strong Arabic tradition, seen in the food, architecture, and features of some of the people. The Moors stayed for as long as the Romans had and left influences as deep. They brought with them Islamic learning and architecture, then the most advanced in the world; new crops, such as cotton, rice, lemons, oranges, figs, and almonds; and revolutionary irrigation techniques, which allowed their crops to flourish.

A Moorish castle, built high above the town of Sintra in the ninth century. Today it is a popular tourist attraction.

THE AGE OF EXPLORATION

Portugal's golden age came in the fifteenth and sixteenth centuries. In this period the country became the world leader in exploration and navigation. An empire was built upon the discoveries that were made in the Far East, India,

11

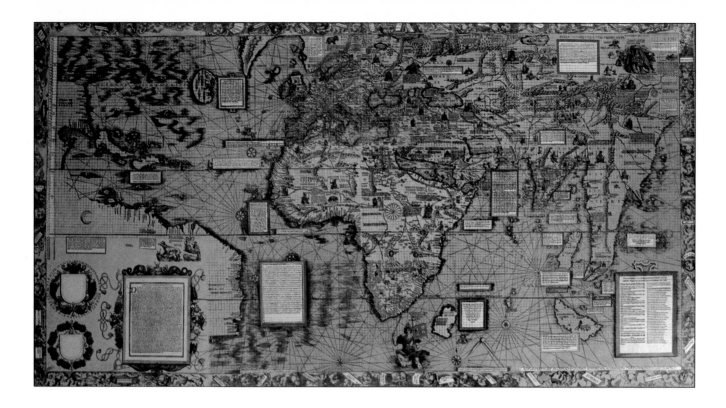

This world map, drawn in 1516, shows the world as it was then known to Portuguese explorers.

Africa, and South America. Prince Henry, called "The Navigator," set up a maritime school at Sagres, on the far southwestern tip of the country. Here mapmakers, navigators, and seamen gathered to exchange ideas and prepare for great voyages of discovery. The wealth that was brought back from these voyages, in the form of spices, gold, silver, and diamonds, made the Portuguese kings the richest in the world.

KEY HISTORICAL DATES

1487: Bartolemeu Dias sailed around the Cape of Good Hope, the southern point of Africa.

1498: Vasco da Gama found a sea route around Africa to India.

1500: Pedro Alvares Cabral crossed the Atlantic and discovered Brazil.

1519: Ferdinand Magellan set off to sail around the world. He died on the voyage, but some of his sailors returned after successfully achieving their aim.

Information from *A Concise History of Portugal*, by David Birmingham

THE DECLINE

The decline of the empire began in 1578. In that year the king and most of his nobles were killed in a disastrous campaign against the Moors in Morocco. Two years later the Spanish invaded a weakened Portugal and took control. They were ejected in 1640. After years of warfare, which left the country impoverished, peace was made in 1688.

While Portugal never regained its vast wealth, many great buildings still exist to remind the people of a proud past. These include Batalha, where Prince Henry is buried, and the monastery of Jeronimos at Belem, near Lisbon. Both of these places today have UNESCO world monument status. They are protected not just for the Portuguese, but for the world.

This is the Monument to the Discoveries. It was built in 1960 to commemorate the 500th anniversary of the death of Prince Henry the Navigator. It is at Belem, near Lisbon.

THE REPUBLIC

By 1910 growing unhappiness with the way the monarchy ruled led to the formation of a republic. The new Republicans began to separate the workings of church and state; they dissolved the monasteries; permitted divorce; reformed secondary education; and held mass literacy classes.

THE GREAT EARTHQUAKE

In 1755 a terrible earthquake struck Lisbon. Most of the city was destroyed and 60,000 people were killed or made homeless. Onto the political scene came one of Portugal's first modernizers: the Marquis of Pombal. He had spent time in London and Vienna and understood modern economics. He helped to rebuild Lisbon and started to rebuild the national economy.

The terrible earthquake of 1755 destroyed most of Lisbon. This picture, drawn by an eyewitness, shows some of the damage.

THE DICTATORSHIP

In 1926, after numerous false starts, changing governments, and in-fighting among Communists, Socialists, and Liberals, a right-wing military coup ended the republic. In 1932, the finance minister became prime minister. He remained in power until 1968 and had considerable influence on the shape of his country's destiny. His name was Antonio Salazar, and he was a shy, old-fashioned, Catholic, financial law lecturer from Coimbra University. He modeled his rule on the fascist regimes of Hitler and Mussolini, though he never followed to their political extremes.

Antonio Salazar dominated Portuguese politics for almost 40 years.

SALAZAR'S POLICIES

Many of the reforms of the liberal nineteenth century and the republic were reversed, setting Portugal back socially and economically. Workers' rights were removed; expenditure on education was cut back; political opposition was repressed; press censorship was introduced; and a police state was set up. Violence was used to silence people who did not like what Salazar was doing.

This fortress was built on the Portuguese coast in the sixteenth century. Over 400 years later it was used by Salazar as a prison to hold people who spoke out against him.

For many years during Salazar's regime, ordinary people's needs were ignored, and city centers were allowed to decay.

Salazar was against economic and industrial modernization and was prepared to allow levels of poverty to sink well below those of any other country in Europe. He increased the power of the church, kept the army on his side, flattered the monarchists, and supported the urban middle classes. The rest of the population—by far the majority —was largely ignored. This majority included the urban workforce and the peasants, and their interests were not looked after for nearly fifty years. Over 85 percent of the population did not have the right to vote. Salazar wanted to keep these people ignorant and poor, but content. His aim was stability, and he used the Church and patriotism as tools to achieve this. And rather than foster enterprise, he encouraged prudence as a way of strengthening the national economy. Salazar's successor and his regime were overthrown in 1974.

The Natural Environment

Sunshine (top) and rainfall (bottom) during June and December.

THE LANDSCAPE

Portugal is roughly the shape of a rectangle and about 347 miles from north to south and 136 miles from east to west. The Atlantic Ocean beats on its coast, bringing a temperate influence to its Mediterranean climate.

The country is cut in half by its main river, the Tagus, and Lisbon is built on its estuary. To the north, 95 percent of the land is over 1,300 feet above sea level. It is an area of high plateaus, deep river valleys, and a few mountain ranges. The south is gentler, flatter, and less varied in appearance. It is a region of plains, hills, and broad river basins. The main rivers run approximately east to west across the country and are more numerous in the north. The coastline, which is 514 miles long, is very varied. It ranges from the imposing cliffs of Cape St. Vincent to the sheltered, sandy beaches of the Algarve.

THE CLIMATE

The Atlantic Ocean has a major influence on Portugal's climate. It has a cooling effect in the hot summer and a warming one in winter. This is because water takes longer to heat up than the

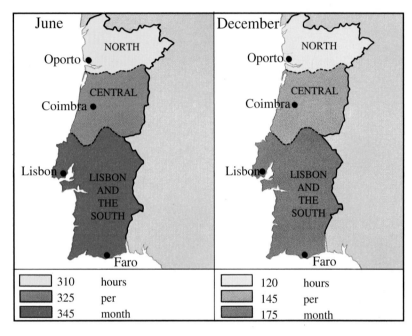

	June	
	310	hours
	325	per
	345	month

	December	
	120	hours
	145	per
	175	month

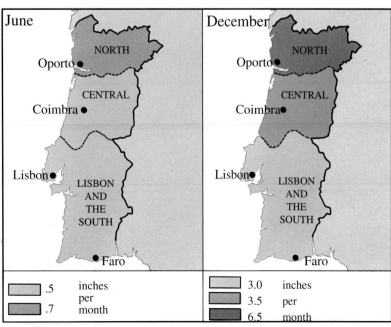

	June	
	.5	inches
		per
	.7	month

	December	
	3.0	inches
	3.5	per
	6.5	month

land, but also takes longer to cool down. The ocean's moderating influence grows weaker as you travel inland. So summers are hotter and winters are colder in the interior.

The winds off the Atlantic also bring clouds and rain, especially to the higher ground of the north. This region has an average annual rainfall of 39 to 58 inches. Most of this arrives in the winter months, between November and March. The Serra de Estrela has the mainland's highest peak, Torre, at 6,500 feet, which is frequently covered in snow in winter, with sub-zero temperatures. In the summer, inland temperatures can reach over 100°F.

The dry interior of the Alentejo. Cork and wheat are grown here in this drought-stricken landscape.

South of the Tagus, the climate becomes more typically Mediterranean. The summers are long, dry, and hot, and the winters shorter, drier, and less cold than in the north. The sea around the Algarve can reach 70°F. Warm, dry

AVERAGE TEMPERATURES			
(in degrees Fahrenheit)	North	Central	South
January	48	54	54
February	50	54	55
March	54	54	55
April	55	61	61
May	59	63	64
June	63	68	70
July	66	70	75
August	68	72	75
September	64	70	72
October	59	64	66
November	54	59	61
December	50	54	55

The dramatic coastline of Cape St. Vincent. This is the most southwesterly point of Portugal and of mainland Europe.

winds frequently blow up from North Africa, very different in character from those off the Atlantic. Drought can become a serious problem inland, often with no rain falling between May and October.

THE VEGETATION

The biggest influences on which plants grow in an area are soil, climate, and altitude. These vary considerably throughout the country, producing a great variety in the vegetation.

In the mountains and high plateaus of the north, the trees most commonly found are birch, chestnut, maple, and oak. Typical ground cover includes gorse, heather, and fern. They are hardier plants, more typical of northern Europe, reflecting the cooler, wetter climate.

In the south, cork oaks, eucalyptus, and olive trees take over. They are more suited to drier, warmer conditions. Vast plains in the Alentejo are covered in this special oak, so it is not surprising that Portugal is the world's largest producer of cork and cork products. It has 50 percent of the world's stock of this tree. The bark is stripped off once every nine or

You can see where this cork tree has been stripped of its bark. This is done about once every nine years, in July or August. Cork is an important product in the Alentejo, where very little else will grow.

These women are harvesting olives. They lay their net on the ground, then knock or shake the olives from the branches.

The Madeira Islands

Funchal, the capital of Madeira. This subtropical island is found off the west coast of Africa.

MADEIRA ISLANDS
Porto Santo
Madeira
ATLANTIC OCEAN
Funchal
0 30 km
0 20 miles
Deserta
Grande

These are found 600 miles from Lisbon, in the Atlantic Ocean. They are volcanic and mountainous. The climate is mild all year round, which makes the islands popular with tourists. The average temperatures vary from 60°F in the winter to 70ºF in the summer. The vegetation is subtropical below 1000 feet. Sugarcane, barbary figs, and bananas were brought to the islands hundreds of years ago, and they grow very happily there. The island is well known for its beautiful flowers and a special wine, called Madeira. The capital is Funchal and the total population is 250,000.

ten years, usually in July or August, and is stacked on trucks and driven to a factory for processing.

Typical shrubs in the south include Mediterranean-type herbs – rosemary, thyme, and lavender. More exotic plants and trees, introduced from tropical or subtropical countries, can also be found in the south. These include carob, figs, almonds, oranges, lemons, and pomegranates.

Agriculture and Fishing

Collecting the maize crop. Many people, especially those of the older generation, are still involved in small-scale farming.

These two industries have been the main occupations of working people of Portugal for centuries. Even the dramatic growth in size of Lisbon and Oporto, from the eighteenth century onward, did little to alter Portugal's rural nature. Food production was still everyone's main concern. Only in the last few decades has this pattern altered significantly. Today only about 11 percent of the workforce is in agriculture and fishing. This is still high for a European country, but in all provinces except the Alentejo, agriculture has been overtaken by industry and services (which includes tourism) in the number of people it employs. The Alentejo is the most farming-based province in Portugal, with almost four times as many people working on the land compared with the rest of the country. It is also the poorest province, with an 11 percent unemployment rate, the highest in the country.

AGRICULTURE

About 60 percent of the land is farmed, but a great deal of the farming is on a small scale. The farmer may grow enough food for the family, with some to sell at a local market, and keep a few animals for milk and meat. This amounts to just about enough to remain above the poverty level. The methods used to cultivate the land are hundreds of years old. In remote communities oxen still pull carts and plows; donkeys are the main

"I lived in Germany for eight years in all. That was where I met my wife. She is Portuguese and was working as a maid in Frankfurt. We both speak very good German after our years there. We saved enough money to return home and buy our own house. I have some land which I farm. We can afford a television and a car and are very happy with our lives. But I'm glad we don't have to go away to another country to work anymore." **– Mario Cavaco, farmer**

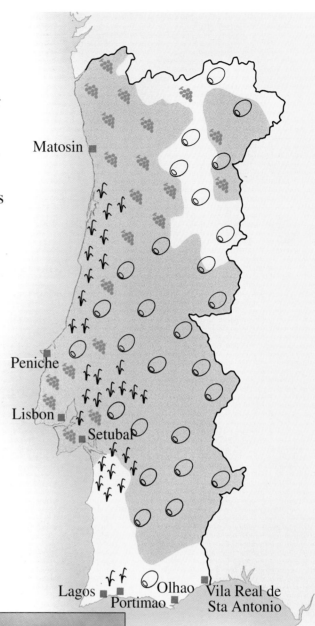

KEY
■ Fishing Port
🍇 Vineyards
⬭ Olive trees
🌾 Rice fields
▨ Cereals

A farmer still uses oxen to pull his cart along this country road.

21

A small farm in the Alentejo

Manuel and Ignacia are in their seventies. They live alone on their 34-acre farm, 3 ½ miles from the nearest village of Santa Clara a Velha. To get there, they have to walk or ride their donkey. A path runs over a hill and connects with a dirt road, which cars can, with difficulty, drive along. They have never been to Lisbon, some three or four hours' drive away. They have never owned a car.

Their farmhouse is in the Alentejo, the largest province in Portugal, and one of the poorest regions of Europe.

"I used to grow a lot more than I do today. The slopes of these hills were covered in wheat once. But we don't need so much now and I'm too old to plow that tough soil." – **Manuel Oliveira, farmer**

It is an agricultural place and has benefited less than any of the other provinces from the economic leap forward. Manuel and Ignacia do not have electricity. Nor do they have piped water or a sewage system.

Ignacia prepares lunch, which she will cook outdoors.

form of transportation and rough paths link farmhouses to dirt roads. Thousands of peasant farmers still live this way. Because of this, Portugal imports $12.3 million worth

Their water comes from a well and their toilet is the great outdoors. They collect gas canisters for their small stove using their ancient donkey. Their lives have changed little over the years, in spite of what has happened to their country. They live in a similar way to their parents and grandparents. And their story is very similar to that of thousands of peasant farmers across the province.

"We have a donkey. We also have chickens and keep a pig which we fatten up. When we slaughter it, it's a day of celebration! We cure the meat and keep it. We used to keep a few cows and sell the calves."
— **Manuel Oliveira**

They have a small vegetable garden, where they grow peppers, tomatoes, potatoes, beans, cabbages, coriander, and parsley. They also grow figs, plums, oranges, olives, pomegranates, and grapes. There is just enough of each to feed the pair. They used to grind their own flour, but today it is brought over the hill in a sack, on the donkey. Every two weeks they bake bread in their outside oven.

Manuel and Felipe are taking the donkey to get a heavy gas cylinder a few miles away.

Their only daughter lives in London with her husband and two children. They come out to the farm on vacation twice a year.

"I used to walk the 3 ½ miles everyday to school. Or maybe sometimes I would stay in the village with friends. I went to school for four years. We worked much harder then than they seem to today. My parents never went to school. They can't read or write."
— **Lena Farren, daughter**

of food and agricultural produce per year, but exports only $7.6 million. Sixteen percent of this is cork; other exports from the land include olive oil, wine, and fruit.

OLD VERSUS NEW

The old, traditional farms and the methods they use seem destined to pass away. Sons and daughters of peasant farmers have been moving away from the land where they were born to take up jobs in towns and cities and in other countries. Paris, for example, has the largest Portuguese population outside Lisbon. Opportunities are open to young people that their parents could never have dreamed of in their youth.

The old and the new are thrown together constantly in modern Portugal. Here a donkey and cart wait patiently alongside a car at some traffic lights.

MODERNIZATION

There are an increasing number of farms being run in a businesslike way. They use modern machinery and fertilizers. The crops they grow are produced for supermarkets or are for export to other countries. These include salad and market garden crops, such as tomatoes, lettuce, peppers, and beans. They are planted in large fields so that harvesting can be more efficient.

Agriculture has benefited from the general improvements made to the country's transportation system. There are new, fast roads and more are being built with investment from the EU. Efficient distribution depots have also been set up, so trucks can now get fresh produce to the towns and cities very quickly. They can also get them to airports, harbors, and on to larger refrigerated trucks for distribution to other countries.

AGRICULTURAL OUTPUT (IN TONS)			
Produce	1990	1991	1992
Wheat	296,300	617,900	300,600
Maize	657,600	648,200	620,000
Rice	156,100	170,500	109,700
Potatoes	1,299,900	1,370,400	1,500,100
Wine (Hl)	10,968,600	9,653,300	7,406,600
Olive oil (Hl)	263,300	668,700	225,000
Cork	173,000	180,000	(not available)
Oranges	167,000	162,000	168,000

NUMBER OF ANIMALS KEPT			
Type	1990	1991	1992
Cattle	1,341,000	1,416,000	1,345,000
Pigs	2,664,000	2,564,000	2,547,000
Sheep	3,360,000	3,380,000	3,348,000

FISHING

The sea continues provide a living for around 30,000 fishermen. Some 17,000 fishing boats are based along Portugal's large coast. They travel as far as Newfoundland and Greenland in their search for cod. About a quarter of a million tons of fish are caught annually and 30 percent of these are sardines from the coastal waters. This fish, along with the tuna caught off the Algarve, makes up the main export of the Portuguese fishing industry. Most are canned in ports such as Peniche, Lagos, Leixoes, and Olhao before being sold. More than 10,000 people are employed in the canning industry, and there are over 100 factories.

Fishermen mend their nets in a village on the Algarve coast.

A deal is struck! The captain of a recently returned fishing boat sells his catch at the port of Ericeira.

The Portuguese love to eat fish, and it is an important part of their national diet. On average, each person eats 17.6 pounds of cod a year. A national cod dish is called "bacalhau." There are said to be 365 ways of cooking it—one for each day of the year! This means that the fishermen can always be sure of selling their catch.

Cod is put out to dry in the sun and the wind. The Portuguese eat more of this fish than any other nation.

"There has always been a fishing village here and it is still one of our finest. The men go to sea and bring home the catch. They can be away for days or weeks sometimes. Then the women make very beautiful and complicated laces, because they have time on their hands. The money we get for them also helps the household economy. Fishing doesn't pay as well as it used to. All these EU restrictions and quotas. We still have lace-making competitions, but it is a dying art. Not many of the young women are taking it up." – Maria Antunes

Industrial Development

This car factory near Lisbon is the result of investment from other European countries.

In the period from 1986 to 1991, Portugal had the fastest-growing economy in Europe. The government successfully attracted investment from abroad to develop its industries. It also got grants from the EU to mend old roads and build new ones. This is continuing today and is very important for the country's development.

Modern new trains and stations, such as those on the line between Sintra and Lisbon, serve commuters and tourists. People are able to travel more easily today, and this encourages trade and industry.

PORTUGAL TODAY

Portugal is still a complex mixture of old and new businesses and industries. The back streets of Lisbon and Oporto are full of small family-run concerns and peddlers. A printer and his apprentice stooping over hot metal and a 100-year-old press is a common sight. So are knife-grinders who walk the streets with their bicycles and grinding stones,

This man is a knife-grinder. He can still make a living in large towns such as Lisbon and Oporto.

Wide avenues lead to expensive shops and fashionable restaurants in one of the wealthier areas of Lisbon.

Portugal is a country of contrasts: close to a shop selling high-tech equipment, you might see a man selling pumpkins on the street.

playing flutes to announce their presence. Cobblers create new shoes out of old; shoeshine rooms pack in ten customers at a time. Alongside these, on fancier streets, are glittering tourist shops, expensive video and camera stores, and jewelers' windows that would not be out of place in Paris, New York, or Frankfurt. On the

SIGNS OF SUCCESS

The single largest foreign investment project came as a joint enterprise between the giant car-making companies Ford and Volkswagen. The company they formed, called AutoEuropa, has built a plant near Setubal, south of Lisbon. It will produce 180,000 cars a year and employ 5,000 people. Total investment is about $3 billion.

outskirts of Lisbon and Oporto there are shanty towns not far from brand-new business parks, which produce electronic parts for multinational companies such as Siemens, Samsung, and Texas Instruments. Industry now employs three times as many people as agriculture and is far more profitable. It also pays better wages.

INVESTMENT

Industry has received money from the government, EU funds, and foreign multinational companies. The government has deliberately gone out to encourage business-people from other countries to build new plants and employ Portuguese workers.

The workforce is becoming increasingly skilled, due to technical and vocational colleges, yet is still among the cheapest to employ in Europe.

THE BENEFITS

The growth in Portugal's industries has brought benefits to the country. In 1986 Portugal had one of the highest rates of unemployment in Europe. Today it has one of the lowest, at around 4 percent. One hundred thousand new jobs have been created each year. Another benefit has been to lift the average income of the population.

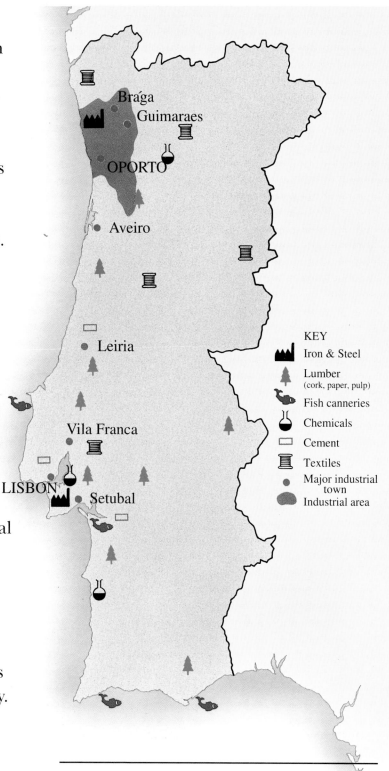

KEY

Iron & Steel

Lumber (cork, paper, pulp)

Fish canneries

Chemicals

Cement

Textiles

Major industrial town

Industrial area

"*Like many people in Portugal today, I have two jobs. I work for the government in Lisbon in a department looking at land use . . . and I have just opened a reproduction antiques shop.*" – **Roberto Ferreira, office worker**

The Gross Domestic Product per person stands at around $8,500. It has increased more than four times since entry into the EU.

Because there are more jobs and better wages, people have more money to spend – on food, clothing, household goods, cars, vacations, and leisure. They also pay higher taxes, which the government can use to continue improving roads, railroads, and schools.

A cafe in Lisbon, where people go to relax and meet friends. Today there are more people with money to spend than ever before.

IMPORTS AND EXPORTS

	Exports (%)	Imports (%)
Agricultural products	7.6	12.1
Minerals and fuels	4.7	8.2
Chemicals, plastics, and rubber	5.3	11.0
Wood, cork, paper, and pulp	10.6	3.4
Textiles and clothing	29.7	10.0
Leather and footwear	9.2	2.2
Metal products	3.5	6.1
Nonmetallic minerals	4.4	1.1
Machinery and electrical goods	14.1	24.3
Vehicles	7.6	16.2
Other products	3.3	5.4

Over 75 percent of these exports go to EU countries — Germany, Spain, France, Italy, and Great Britain. Over 71 percent of its imports come from the same source – the EU.

Portugal imports far more goods than it exports. Also, it exports things that are cheap and imports things that are expensive. This is not good for the economy. Opening new plants that produce expensive goods for export (like the automobile factory in Setubal) will help to change this.

Tourism

Lord Byron, the famous poet, stayed in Sintra in 1809 and wrote about the area in a letter home:

"It (Sintra) contains beauties of every description, natural and artificial. Palaces and gardens rising in the midst of rocks, cataracts and precipices; convents on stupendous heights, a distant view of the sea and the Tagus . . . It unites in itself all the wildness of the Western Highlands with the verdure of the South of France."

Portugal has a long tradition of tourism, going back to the eighteenth century. It was a place where wealthy Europeans on the Grand Tour went, after Italy, France, and Spain.

Mass tourism took off in the middle of the 1960s. Northern Europeans, with money from booming economies, went looking for southern European sunshine and warm seas. Portugal was "discovered" by emerging tour operators. The number of people visiting the country has been steadily increasing ever since.

The Palacio da Pena, overlooking Sintra and the beautiful surrounding countryside. It was built in the 1840s and has become a major tourist site.

The popular Algarve coast at the height of the tourist season.

MARKET SHARE

By the early 1990s, nearly 20 million tourists a year were choosing Portugal as their vacation destination although only 200,000 were U.S. tourists. Over the last ten years the average growth in the number of visitors has been over 11 percent each year. This is far above the rate for Europe as a whole (3.5 percent per year) and the world tourist market (4.2 percent). In the same period, statistics show that Portugal's share of the European tourist market has more than doubled.

DEPENDENCY ON TOURISM

This pattern reflects the growth of the economy as a whole. Starting from a low base, the 1980s saw a boom and growth rate that outstripped other countries. But the overall number of tourists is still modest when compared with giants like France (over 50 million a year), and Spain and Italy (over 30 million each). However, perhaps the most interesting fact is that the income from those 20 million tourists is far more important to the Portuguese economy than the income from the greater number of visitors to France, Spain, or Italy. It makes up four percent of the Gross Domestic Product, two times higher than in France and Italy.

Portugal is more dependent on the tourist sector than other tourist destinations in Europe. Tourism is an unreliable source of income because it depends upon the economies of other countries. In healthy economies, people have spare cash and will spend some of it on travel. In times of recession, as have been experienced over the past few years, one of the first things people cut back on is foreign vacations. The more dependent a country is on that income, the more drastic the consequences can be. But Portugal is still a cheap place to visit for most people and is winning tourists from other, more expensive destinations. So far the recession has not affected Portugal's tourist industry too badly.

WHERE THEY COME FROM	
Country of origin	(% of Portugal's tourists)
Spain	44%
Great Britain	14%
Germany	9%
France	7%
The Netherlands	4%
Italy	3%
United States	1%
Other	18%

33

These two ladies run small hotels in Nazare, on the coast. They will make their money in the busy summer months, and close down in winter.

WHY THEY COME

Portugal is relatively easy to reach from other European countries. There are international airports at Lisbon, Oporto, and Faro; people also come by ship and by train; and of course there are roads, which are being improved and extended all the time. Tourism has encouraged road development. This can be seen by the new, high-standard roads found just inland from the Algarve, Portugal's main tourist area. In the fall and winter these roads are almost empty. In the summer they carry tourist traffic to and from the busy Algarve coast. Portugal has the lowest car rental rates in Europe. This is a deliberate policy, to encourage people to come to the country and also to get around and spend their money in different areas.

Portugal is also one of the cheapest countries in Europe for everyday necessities. Eating out, for example, costs a fraction of what it does in France, Great Britain, or the United States.

Portugal offers traditional beach vacations at low cost on the Algarve and west coast. Plenty of resorts have been developed to a high standard of luxury and convenience. Many have golf and tennis facilities. Swimming, surfing, and sunbathing are popular pastimes. There are also very good facilities for business conferences, where work and pleasure can be combined. Lisbon and Oporto are cities of international standing, with many museums, galleries, and historical buildings to visit.

Lisbon was named the 1994 European City of Culture. It follows Athens, Florence, Amsterdam, Dublin, Berlin, Paris, Glasgow, Madrid, and Antwerp. Its 7500-foot-long suspension bridge, Ponte 25 de Abril, spans the Tagus River, linking the north with the south. It lets people travel all the way from the beautiful wooded hills and summer palaces of ancient kings and queens in Sintra to the beaches of the Algarve.

Portugal is also a land rich in history, of which it is very proud. There are hundreds of Moorish and Christian castles dotting the landscape from north to south. Monuments, cathedrals, a few mosques, palaces, and Roman temples dot the countryside.

A life-size bronze of a poet sits outside a cafe in Lisbon.

TOURISM AND THE ECONOMY

Over 250,000 people nationwide are directly employed in the tourist industry. This is around five percent of the working population. The income represents 6.5 percent of the GNP, around $3.6 billion. Lisbon and its surroundings and the Algarve are the main areas of tourist activity. Here, tourism and other service industries account for over half the jobs, with industry and agriculture following behind. Where Portugal once looked for wealth from its colonies in India, the Far East, Africa, and South America, it now looks much closer to home – to the neighboring European Union countries.

"I remember when people in the Algarve were so poor, we used to cross into the Alentejo to find work on the farms. That's maybe 40 years ago. Today the situation is reversed. The Alentejo is poor and the young people have left their parents' farms to find work in the tourist season on the Algarve coast. There is plenty of money about if you know how to find it."
– Manolo Perao, hotel waiter, Albufeira

Tourism on the coast of Portugal has created many jobs. These waiters will earn a lot of money over the summer months.

Education and the People

Portugal is a Catholic country. Large, wealthy churches are found everywhere, reflecting the power and prestige of the clergy.

The Parliament building in Lisbon, where politicians meet to discuss the running of the country.

CHURCH AND STATE

For hundreds of years education was in the hands of the church and was only for the few. It did not come under state control until the middle of the eighteenth century. The church deliberately kept out any new thoughts or theories that might lead the people to question its power. Science, philosophy, and mathematics were among the censored subjects. This held back progress in education for generations.

EDUCATIONAL REFORM

Education for all did not come about until after the 1974 democratic revolution. Reforms were made to counteract one of the worst literacy records in Europe.

The number of illiterate adults is now under 20 percent, but this is still extremely high by European standards.

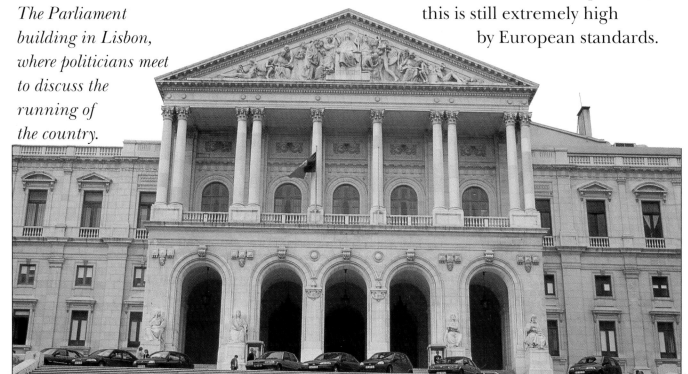

*"We have three children and have made sure that they look after their books, which are expensive. When one child has finished with a book, it is passed on to the younger ones who will need it." – **Silvia Lopez, mother, Oporto***

The situation has not been helped by the fact that schools in the past often did not supply the books needed for study. Poorer parents would have to save hard to buy the necessary reading material. The library system is not very developed, even today.

STRUCTURE AND ORGANIZATION

Almost 20 percent of Portugal's population is under 25 years old. This is 2 million people – the largest group in the country – in need of education. The government has stated that "education will be given national priority." The Ministry of Education is responsible for making the policy to improve schools and for finding the money to carry it out. Education is compulsory and free for all from the ages of 6 to 13 years who have enrolled since 1987. Preschool (3 to 6 years old) is available but optional. Optional secondary school is three years (14 to 16) and is also free. For children 10 to 13 old years living in remote rural areas there is provision for education out of school using audiovisual aids.

Children from remote areas often have to travel long distances to attend school. This school in Alentejo is in the largest, poorest, and least populated region of Portugal.

HIGHER EDUCATION

Beyond school there are choices in higher education.
Technical and vocational courses are run for both full- and
part-time students. The courses are practical and aimed at
getting the students jobs in such areas as engineering,
carpentry, building, mechanics, accounting, and tourism.
Although the qualifications relate directly to jobs, they can
also be used to gain entrance into one of the country's 14
universities. Coimbra University dates from the thirteenth
century; those in Lisbon and Oporto were founded in 1911,
after the Republican Revolution; and others have since
opened in more remote areas, as well as on the islands of
the Azores and Madeira, to serve the needs of local people.

Coimbra University was founded in the thirteenth century and is one of the oldest in Europe.

EDUCATION: FACTS AND FIGURES			
	Actual number	% of the population	Average pupil: teacher ratio
Children at primary school	1,400,000	14%	20:1
Children at secondary school	850,000	8.5%	13:1
Students in higher education	250,000	2.5%	8:1

ADULT EDUCATION

In 1979 a law was passed to improve basic education and literacy for adults. This was because there were many adults who had never been to school. A document called the National Plan for Adult Basic Education was drawn up and approved. Educational law today gives all adults the right to increase their knowledge and develop their abilities.

THE FUTURE

The government has set the year 2000 as the target date for overcoming all the inherited problems of a poor educational system. So far hundreds of schools have been built throughout the country and more are to come. The welfare of future generations in the area of education will remain high on the political agenda.

"We have a lot of young people in our country. This is why education is so important. To be able to survive and develop further in the modern world we need to make sure that our schools and universities are turning out enough businesspeople, engineers, chemists, bankers, and so on." – **Ana Covilha**

Future Challenges

Portugal is a country that has undergone more changes than most others in Europe over the last ten years. After hundreds of years of neglect and underdevelopment, it has been put on a fast track to modernize itself.

RECENT ADVANCES

The late twentieth century has seen a return to democracy and full integration with the European Union. Outside investment and money from tourism have combined with a strong political will to enable the nation to increase its wealth. Multinational companies have set up plants, industry has expanded and diversified, and exports have increased. These advances have been supported by a policy of improving communications and transportation, especially roads and telecommunications. The lack of natural energy resources has partly been offset by the construction of about 60 hydroelectric dams, which produce millions of kilowatts

This hydroelectric dam has been built across the Douro River. Dams are an important source of energy.

Rural Regeneration in the Algarve

It has been recognized for a long time that inland rural communities have been suffering from stagnation and decline. There are very few opportunities for people in the countryside, so the young people leave to find work elsewhere.

"This area had been declining for years. No one came here. We have seen how the coast has changed since the 1960s, but we remained poor and backward and forgotten. But now we have the project. Let's hope it works."
—Henrique de Sousa, retired

To help reverse this trend, rural regeneration projects have been set up. They are backed by local and national government and by the EU. One such project has been set up in the Algarve, and is called the RADIAL scheme.

The project is there to help local communities to use their own skills, adapting them to the modern world,

Traditional crafts, such as lace-making, are being encouraged by government funded projects. These projects are helping to boost the economies of poor agricultural regions by finding outlets for their products in towns and cities.

of power and now supply 50 percent of the nation's needs. So although Portugal was one of the last countries in Europe to modernize, it has done so with great determination and with the backing of the European Union.

Ceramic pots for sale at a market

and to the tourist industry. Local skills that can benefit are honey, wax, and candlestick making; traditional candy making; cork products; aromatic and medicinal herbs; handicrafts in wool and linen; basket-making and embroidery; ceramics; and traditional liqueur making.

The aim is to make small businesses successful, which will encourage people to stay in the region. Money coming into the communities will stimulate other forms of employment, such as house-building, repairs, and decorating.

"I have been employed by the RADIAL project to teach woodwork. We want to use the traditional skills that people once had around here and gear them toward the tourist market. Souvenirs made out of wood sell well down on the coast." –Joao Ferreira, RADIAL worker

SOCIAL BENEFITS
These advances have enabled the general standard of living to rise considerably. Inflation is low and so is unemployment, at 4.7 percent. Educational standards are rising and illiteracy is being tackled. Health and health care

43

The church still plays a very important role in the community. Many people use it as their social center.

have improved considerably, as has social security. Before the revolution of 1974, this was left to a haphazard system in which individual companies used funds to help sick employees. This was made into one national fund and benefits were increased. Today the system provides old age, disability, death, sickness, and maternity benefits.

THE ROLE OF THE CHURCH

Help for the poor and unemployed has traditionally been provided for by the twin institutions of church and family. These institutions still have a great deal of power, especially in the more conservative north and in the farming communities. But there is increasing pressure for the state to take control and for the role of the church to be minimized.

44

Changes in Portugal have not come without some cost. On the economic side, the country still imports far more than it exports. This means that there is a trade deficit. Portugal also has a very large national debt, and borrowing money to develop is a costly business because of interest payments. On the social level, there are growing gaps between town and country. Lisbon, Oporto, and other towns and cities are generally benefiting from progress. But huge areas of land in the countryside are being emptied of young people, leaving only the older generations. The fate of the countryside is of great concern to the government. The lifestyles and expectations of the young have changed greatly from their parents', let alone those of their grandparents'. They now inhabit a very different world.

Portugal is living through these changes and upheavals now. But it is a country with a stronger sense of history than most. This strong sense of the past may help keep the new Portugal in balance. The church and the family are still very powerful and will, the government hopes, continue to play a part in the lives of the young people, keeping them in contact with old traditions and values.

The family is still an important institution in Portugal. It is not uncommon to see extended families – parents, grandparents, and children – all living under the same roof.

45

Glossary

Censorship Preventing the publication, or presentation, of media (books and films, for example) that are considered obscene or unacceptable.

Democracy A political system in which the people vote for their government.

Dictatorship A political system in which one person or government rules without having been voted in by the people. Dictatorships do not allow people to disagree with their views.

Empire A country or countries ruled by a single authority.

European Union Countries in western Europe who have decided to work together for trade and political purposes. At present, these countries are: Belgium, Denmark, France, Germany, Greece, Ireland, Italy, Luxembourg, The Netherlands, Portugal, Spain, and the United Kingdom.

Financial Aid Giving money to help a country in need.

Gross National Product The total amount of goods and services produced by a country in any one year.

Gross Domestic Product The total amounts of goods and services produced by a country in a year, with the income from foreign investment taken away.

Hydroelectric The generation of electricity by water pressure.

Illiterate Unable to read or write.

Investment Money that is put into a business or industry.

Irrigation Water brought to a dry area by means of channels or canals.

Legacy Something handed down or received from an ancestor or predecessor.

Liberalism A movement that grew in Europe in the 18th and 19th centuries. It argued for freedom and equality among all people.

Maritime Related to the sea.

National Debt The total amount of money a government has borrowed.

Policy A plan of action.

Province A region within a country. Provinces often have their own traditions and local government.

Recession A temporary drop in a country's monetary exchange.

Regime Another word for government. It is often used when the government is especially strict, such as those of Hitler, Mussolini, and Stalin.

Republic A type of government that does not have a king or queen.

Rural Regeneration The renewal of destroyed land for regrowth, agriculture, or industrial use.

Sanitation The use of proper sanitary arrangements – for example, keeping water clean for drinking, or removing sewage cleanly to protect health.

Service Industry An industry that provides a service, such as transportation or entertainment, rather than goods.

Sewage System An underground drain for receiving and carrying away dirty water and waste matter from houses and streets.

Temperate A climate that is not too hot or too cold.

Trade Deficit The dollar amount by which a country's imports exceed its exports.

Vocational Course An educational course that prepares the person taking it for a trade or profession.

UNESCO United Nations Educational, Scientific, and Cultural Organization. Its headquarters are in Paris, France.

Further Information

BOOKS

Chrisp, Peter. *The Search for the East.* Exploration & Encounters. New York: Thomson Learning, 1993.

Economically Developing Countries. Series. New York: Thomson Learning.

Moore, Richard. *Portugal.* World in View. Austin, TX: Raintree/Steck-Vaughn, 1992.

Twist, Clint. *Magellan and Da Gama.* Beyond the Horizons. Austin, TX: Raintree/Steck-Vaughn, 1994.

USEFUL ADDRESSES

Embassy of Portugal
2125 Kalorama Rd., N.W.
Washington, D.C. 20009
(202) 234-3800

The Portuguese Tourism Office
590 Fifth Ave.
New York NY 10036
(212) 354-4403

The President of Portugal
Presidencia da Republica
Palacio de Belem
1300 Lisbon
Portugal

You can get free information on all aspects of Portugal by writing to these addresses.

All the boxed information in the text has been provided by The Portuguese Trade and Tourism Office and The Portuguese Embassy.

PICTURE ACKNOWLEDGMENTS
The publishers would like to thank the following for allowing their photographs to be reproduced in this book: AutoEuropa, Lisbon: 27 (top); Camera Press: 19, 26 (bottom), 28 (top); Cephas: Title page, 7, 11, 39, 41; Neil Champion: Contents page, 4, 6, 8, 10, 15 (both), 17 (both), 18 (both), 22, 23, 26 (top), 27 (bottom), 28 (bottom), 35, 37 (bottom), 38 (bottom), 42, 45; Chapel Studios: 30; Mary Evans: 12, 13 (bottom); Eye Ubiquitous: 13 (top), 44; Robert Harding: Cover; Tony Stone Worldwide: 21, 25, 43; Topham Picture Source: 14, 20, 24, 31, 32, 34, 36, 37; Wayland Picture Library: 9, 38 (top) 40. Maps were provided by Peter Bull.

Index

The figures in **bold** refer to photographs and maps.